Animal Life Cycles

Anita Ganeri

Heinemann Library
Chicago, Illinois

2005 Heinemann Library
a division of Reed Elsevier Inc.
Chicago, Illinois

Customer Service 888-454-2279

Visit our website at www.heinemannlibrary.com

Designed by Jo Malivoire
Printed and bound in China by South China Printing Company

09 08 07 06 05
10 9 8 7 6 5 4 3 2 1

Library of Congress Cataloging-in-Publication Data
Ganeri, Anita, 1961-
   Animal life cycles / Anita Ganeri.
      p. cm. — (Nature's patterns)
   Includes bibliographical references and index.
   ISBN 1-4034-5894-4 ((hc)) — ISBN 1-4109-1317-1 ((pbk.))
   1. Animal life cycles—Juvenile literature. I. Title. II. Series.
   QL49.G2419 2004
   571.8'1—dc22
                                   2004007460

Acknowledgments
The author and publishers are grateful to the following for permission to reproduce copyright
material: p. **4** Mike Jones/Frank Lane Picture Agency/Corbis; p. **5** Sygma/Andanson
James/Corbis; pp. **6**, **23** Royalty Free/Corbis; pp. **7**, **8** Harcourt; pp. **8**, **9** Photodisc; p. **11**
Stephen Dalton/NHPA; p. **13** Anthony Bannister/ NHPA; p. **15** Max Gibbs/OSF; p. **17** Simon
Booth/NHPA; p. **19** Shaen Adey/Gallo Images/Corbis; p. **21** Maurizio Lanini/Corbis; pp. **25**,
27 D Parer and E Parer-Cook/Ardea; p. **26** Robert Thompson/NHPA; p. **28** Hellio and Van
Ingen/NHPA; p. **29** Anup Shah/Nature Photo Library.

Cover photograph of a baby giraffe and its mother by Steve Bloom.

Every effort has been made to contact copyright holders of any material reproduced in this book.
Any omissions will be rectified in subsequent printings if notice is given to the publisher.

Some words are shown in bold, **like this**. You can find out what
they mean by looking in the glossary.

Contents

Nature's Patterns

Nature is always changing. Many of the changes that happen follow a **pattern.** This means that they happen over and over again.

A duckling **hatches** from an egg. This is the start of its life cycle.

The different times in an animal's life are linked together in a pattern called a life cycle.

Animal life cycles follow a pattern. Animals are born, grow up, have babies, get old, and die.

Animals and Babies

Many animals have babies when they grow up. Then the babies grow up and have their own young. So, the life cycle **pattern** begins again.

A cat's babies are called kittens.

A caterpillar is the baby of a moth or butterfly.

As they get older, animals grow and change. Some baby animals look like tiny copies of their parents. Others look very different from their parents.

7

Animal Groups

There are many different groups of animals. You can see animals from six of the groups here. These groups are **insects,** fish, **amphibians, reptiles,** birds, and **mammals.**

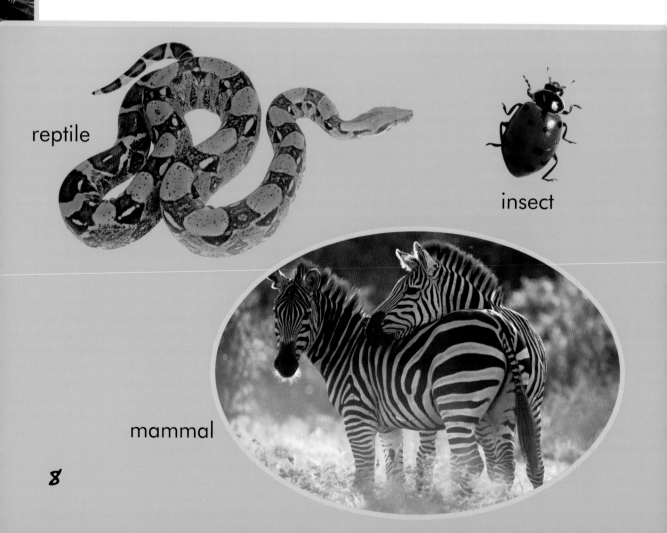

reptile

insect

mammal

fish

bird

amphibian

The animals in each group share many of the same **features.** For example, all birds have feathers and beaks. The animals in each group also have life cycles that are alike.

9

Insect changes

There are two kinds of **insect** life cycles. In the first kind, a female insect lays lots of eggs. The eggs **hatch** into babies that look like little adults.

adult grasshopper laying eggs

grasshoppers hatching from eggs

A grasshopper goes through different stages as it changes into an adult.

adult grasshopper

young grasshoppers

After it has molted, a young locust looks like a little adult.

As the young insect grows, its old skin splits and falls off. This is called **molting**. There is a new, bigger skin underneath the old one.

11

Amazing Changes

In the second kind of **insect** life cycle, the female also lays eggs. When an egg **hatches,** the baby does not look like the adults. It is called a **larva.**

These are the different stages in a butterfly's life cycle. An egg turns into a larva, then a pupa, and then an adult.

larva hatching from an egg

adult butterfly laying eggs

larva (caterpillar)

hatching from a pupa

pupa

These bees are each in their own pupa. They are changing to become adult bees.

The young insect eats and grows. Then it spins a cover around its body. This is called a **pupa.** Inside the pupa, the larva's body changes into an adult.

13

fishy Lives

A baby fish **hatches** from an egg. The female lays her eggs in the water. Some fish lay thousands of eggs, but they do not take care of the babies when they hatch.

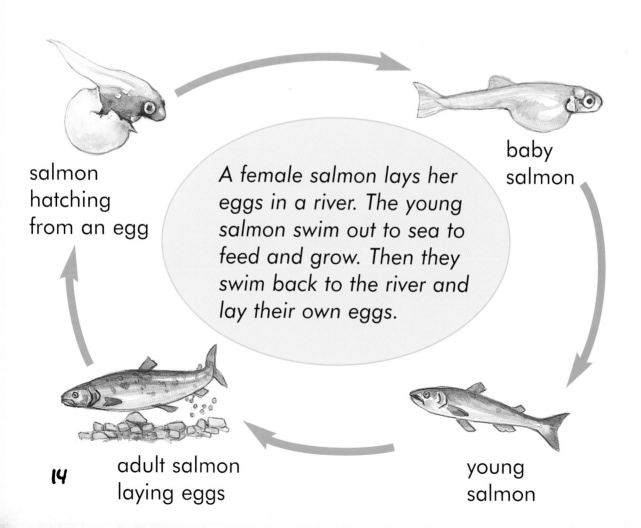

salmon hatching from an egg

baby salmon

A female salmon lays her eggs in a river. The young salmon swim out to sea to feed and grow. Then they swim back to the river and lay their own eggs.

adult salmon laying eggs

young salmon

When a baby fish hatches, it looks like a little adult. It swims around looking for food. The baby grows quickly and becomes an adult fish.

*A young fish grows into an adult and lays its own eggs. Then the life cycle **pattern** begins again.*

15

Frogs and Toads

Frogs and toads are **amphibians.** They are born in water. The female lays lots of jelly-like eggs.

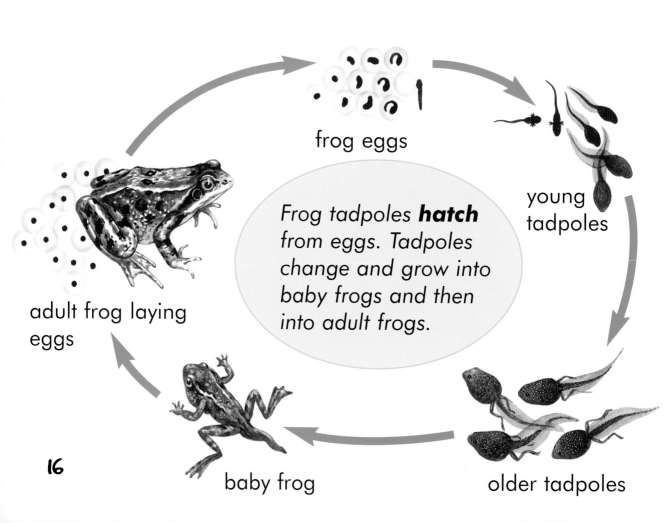

frog eggs

young tadpoles

Frog tadpoles *hatch* from eggs. Tadpoles change and grow into baby frogs and then into adult frogs.

adult frog laying eggs

baby frog

older tadpoles

Toads change from eggs into tadpoles and then into young toads.

Baby frogs and toads look very different from their parents. They swim like fish and are called tadpoles. Soon they start to grow legs and look like little adults.

Reptile Babies

Animals such as snakes, crocodiles, alligators, tortoises, and turtles are **reptiles.** Most reptiles lay eggs with tough, leathery shells. They lay their eggs on land in holes or nests.

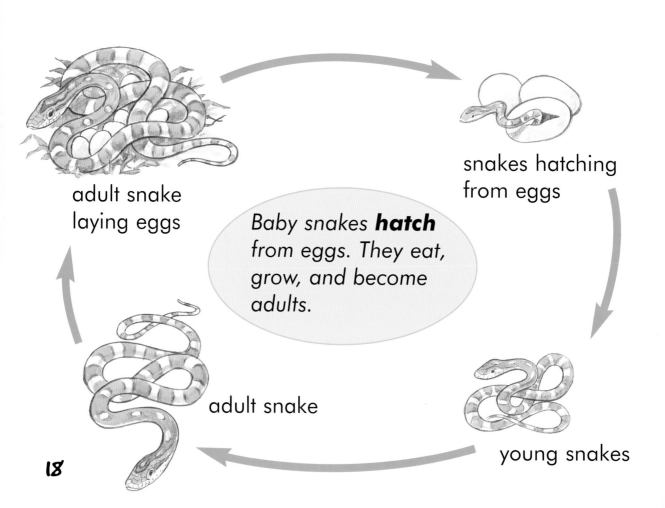

adult snake laying eggs

snakes hatching from eggs

*Baby snakes **hatch** from eggs. They eat, grow, and become adults.*

adult snake

young snakes

An adult crocodile with its newly hatched baby.

When baby reptiles hatch, they look like their parents. They eat and grow to become adult size. When they are adults, the females can lay their own eggs.

19

Chicks and Nests

A female bird lays eggs with hard shells. Most birds lay their eggs in nests to keep them safe. A parent sits on the eggs to keep them warm.

chick hatching from egg

chick

egg laid by an adult chicken

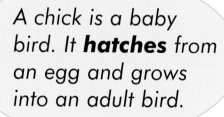

A chick is a baby bird. It **hatches** from an egg and grows into an adult bird.

adult chicken

young chicken

As a chick gets older, it learns how to fly.

Baby birds are called chicks. They hatch from eggs. Their parents bring them food and care for them until they can take care of themselves.

21

Mammal Lives

Guinea pigs, dogs, and human beings are all **mammals.** Most baby mammals grow inside their mother's body. They look like their parents when they are born.

adult and newborn guinea pig

baby guinea pigs

A baby guinea pig looks like its parents when it is born. It grows bigger and becomes an adult.

adult guinea pig

young guinea pig

Female mammals feed their babies milk.

Most mammals are caring parents. Some take care of their young for a few weeks or months. Others care for their young for many years.

Eggs and Pouches

Two kinds of **mammals** have different life cycles. A duck-billed platypus lays eggs with soft shells. When a baby platypus **hatches** from its egg, it feeds on its mother's milk.

A platypus spends a lot of time in water.

Female kangaroos have pouches on their fronts. A baby kangaroo is tiny and helpless. It crawls up its mother's fur into her pouch. There it drinks her milk and grows bigger.

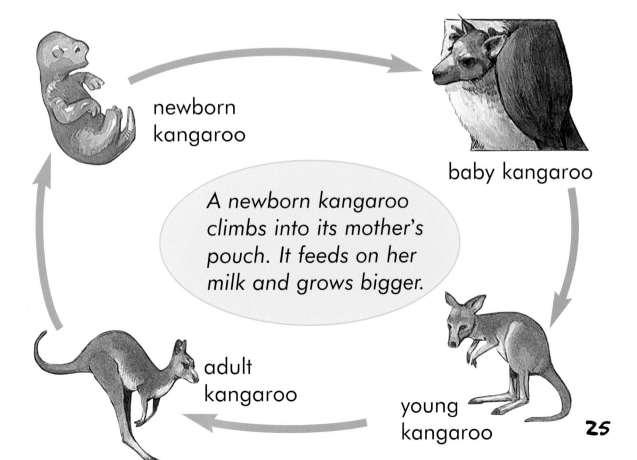

newborn kangaroo

baby kangaroo

A newborn kangaroo climbs into its mother's pouch. It feeds on her milk and grows bigger.

adult kangaroo

young kangaroo

Animal Life Spans

An animal's life span is how long an animal lives for. Some animals have very short lives. An adult mayfly only lives for about a day. It lays its eggs and then dies.

Like many **insects,** this mayfly has a short life span.

Mammals and some reptiles, like tortoises, have long life spans.

Some animals live for a long time. Elephants can live until they are 70 years old. Some kinds of tortoise can live for about 150 years.

27

Old Age

At the end of their lives, animals die. But many wild animals do not die of old age. They are killed by other animals or **diseases.** Some **starve** if they cannot find enough food.

This fox has killed a bird to eat.

This baby orangutan will grow into an adult. It may have babies of its own one day.

An animal's death is not the end of the life-cycle **pattern.** Baby animals grow into adults and have babies of their own. In this way, the pattern happens over and over again.

fact file

Animals have different life spans. Here are some of the longest known life spans for different kinds of animals:

Giant tortoise	177 years
Human being	125 years
Asian elephant	78 years
American alligator	66 years
Jewel beetle	47 years
Polar bear	41 years
Eastern gray kangaroo	28 years
Bird-eating spider	28 years
Sea star (starfish)	7 years
Monarch butterfly	9 months
Housefly	29 days

Glossary

amphibian animal that lives in water and on land

disease sickness

feature what an animal looks like, how it lives, and what it eats

hatch break out of an egg

insect small animal with six legs

larva insect baby

mammal warm-blooded animal with hair that feeds its babies milk

molt split and fall off

pattern something that happens over and over again

pupa silk cover that a larva makes before becoming an adult

reptile animal with scaly skin

starve die because there is not enough to eat

More Books to Read

Fridell, Ron and Patricia Walsh. *Life Cycle of a Spider*. Chicago: Heinemann Library, 2002.

Royston, Angela. *Life Cycle of a Chicken*. Chicago: Heinemann Library, 2001.

Royston, Angela. *Life Cycle of a Dog*. Chicago: Heinemann Library, 2000.

Index